Potatoes With Sea Salt And Rosemary

Ingredients:

2 lbs baby potatoes
2 tbsp olive oil
2 tbsp fresh rosemary, finely chopped
1 tbsp coarse sea salt
Freshly ground black pepper, to taste

Instructions:

Preheat your oven to 400°F (200°C).
Scrub the potatoes and pat them dry with a paper towel.
In a large bowl, toss the potatoes with olive oil, rosemary, sea salt, and black pepper until evenly coated.
Arrange the potatoes in a single layer on a baking sheet lined with parchment paper.
Roast the potatoes in the preheated oven for 30-35 minutes, or until they are crispy on the outside and tender on the inside.
Once the potatoes are done, remove them from the oven and let them cool for a few minutes before serving.
Transfer the potatoes to a serving dish and sprinkle with additional sea salt and black pepper, if desired.
Serve the potatoes as a side dish or snack, garnished with fresh rosemary sprigs. Enjoy!

Spring Rolls

Ingredients:

12-14 spring roll wrappers
2 cups shredded cabbage
1 cup shredded carrot
1 red bell pepper, thinly sliced
1/2 cup sliced scallions
1/4 cup chopped fresh cilantro
1/4 cup chopped fresh mint
1/4 cup chopped fresh basil
1/4 cup tamari or soy sauce
2 tbsp rice vinegar
1 tbsp maple syrup
2 tsp grated ginger
2 cloves garlic, minced
1 tbsp cornstarch
2 tbsp water
Oil for frying

Instructions:

In a large bowl, combine the shredded cabbage, shredded carrot, red bell pepper, scallions, cilantro, mint, and basil.
In a separate bowl, whisk together the tamari, rice vinegar, maple syrup, grated ginger, and minced garlic until well combined.
Pour the tamari mixture over the vegetable mixture and toss until everything is coated evenly.
In a small bowl, whisk together the cornstarch and water to make a slurry.
Lay a spring roll wrapper on a clean surface and place 2-3 tablespoons of the vegetable mixture in the center.
Fold the bottom of the wrapper up over the filling, then fold in the sides and roll the wrapper up tightly. Use the cornstarch slurry to seal the edges of the wrapper.
Repeat with the remaining wrappers and filling.
Heat the oil in a deep skillet or wok over medium-high heat.
Once the oil is hot, add the spring rolls in batches and fry for 2-3 minutes on each side, or until they are golden brown and crispy.
Use a slotted spoon to transfer the spring rolls to a paper towel-lined plate to drain off any excess oil.
Serve the spring rolls hot, with your favorite dipping sauce. Enjoy!

he Vegan Recipes Cookbook for Kids is a fun and engaging cookbook that introduces young chefs to the world of plant-based cooking. This cookbook is packed with simple and easy-to-follow recipes that are perfect for kids to make on their own or with the help of a parent or caregiver.

From breakfast smoothie bowls and colorful salads to hearty stews and sweet treats, the Vegan Recipes Cookbook for Kids offers a variety of delicious and nutritious vegan dishes. Each recipe is designed with children in mind, with step-by-step instructions and helpful tips for getting them involved in the cooking process.

In addition to recipes, this cookbook includes information on the benefits of a plant-based diet, as well as tips for making the transition to veganism. It also features colorful illustrations and playful design elements to engage children and make cooking a fun and interactive experience.

The Vegan Recipes Cookbook for Kids is perfect for families who want to incorporate more plant-based foods into their diets, or for those who are already vegan and looking for new and exciting recipe ideas. With this cookbook, children can learn about the importance of healthy eating and gain confidence in the kitchen as they prepare delicious and nutritious vegan meals.

Hummus

Ingredients:

1 can (15 oz) of chickpeas, drained and rinsed
1/4 cup tahini
1/4 cup lemon juice
2 garlic cloves, minced
1/2 tsp ground cumin
1/4 tsp paprika
1/4 cup olive oil
Salt to taste
2-3 tbsp water, as needed

Instructions:

In a food processor, combine the chickpeas, tahini, lemon juice, minced garlic, cumin, paprika, and salt.
Process the mixture until it's smooth and creamy, scraping down the sides of the bowl as needed.
While the food processor is still running, slowly pour in the olive oil through the feed tube. This will help emulsify the mixture and make it even creamier.
If the hummus is too thick, add water one tablespoon at a time until it reaches your desired consistency.
Taste the hummus and adjust the seasoning as needed with more salt, lemon juice, or spices.
Serve the hummus with pita bread, veggies, or your favorite dipping vehicle. Enjoy!

Vegan Pulled Jackfruit

Ingredients:

2 cans (20 oz) young green jackfruit in water or brine
1 tbsp olive oil
1 onion, chopped
3 garlic cloves, minced
1/4 cup tomato paste
1/4 cup apple cider vinegar
1/4 cup maple syrup
2 tbsp soy sauce
2 tbsp smoked paprika
1 tsp ground cumin
1/2 tsp chili powder
1/4 tsp cayenne pepper (optional)
Salt and black pepper to taste

Instructions:

Drain and rinse the jackfruit, then cut off the hard core and discard it.
Use your fingers or a fork to shred the jackfruit into small pieces that resemble pulled pork.
Heat the olive oil in a large skillet over medium-high heat.
Add the chopped onion and sauté for 2-3 minutes, or until it's soft and translucent.
Add the minced garlic and sauté for an additional 1-2 minutes, or until it's fragrant.
Add the tomato paste, apple cider vinegar, maple syrup, soy sauce, smoked paprika, ground cumin, chili powder, and cayenne pepper (if using). Stir well to combine.
Add the shredded jackfruit to the skillet and stir until it's coated evenly with the sauce.
Reduce the heat to medium-low, cover the skillet, and let the jackfruit simmer for 15-20 minutes, or until it's tender and the sauce has thickened.
Use a fork to mash the jackfruit slightly, which will give it a more pulled texture.
Season the pulled jackfruit with salt and black pepper to taste.
Serve the pulled jackfruit hot, with your favorite toppings such as avocado, cilantro, red onion, or vegan sour cream. Enjoy!

Lemon Cake

Ingredients:

2 cups all-purpose flour
1 1/2 tsp baking powder
1/2 tsp baking soda
1/4 tsp salt
1/2 cup vegan butter, softened
1 cup granulated sugar
1/2 cup unsweetened applesauce
1/2 cup non-dairy milk
1/4 cup fresh lemon juice
2 tbsp lemon zest

For the lemon glaze:

1 cup powdered sugar
1/4 cup fresh lemon juice
1 tbsp lemon zest

Instructions:

Preheat your oven to 350°F (180°C).

Grease a 9-inch cake pan with cooking spray or vegan butter, and dust with flour.
In a medium bowl, whisk together the flour, baking powder, baking soda, and salt.
In a large mixing bowl, cream the vegan butter and sugar together until light and fluffy.
Add the applesauce, non-dairy milk, lemon juice, and lemon zest to the butter mixture, and mix until well combined.
Slowly add the dry ingredients to the wet mixture, and mix until just combined.
Pour the batter into the prepared cake pan, and smooth the top with a spatula.
Bake for 35-40 minutes, or until a toothpick inserted in the center of the cake comes out clean.
Allow the cake to cool in the pan for 10 minutes, then transfer it to a wire rack to cool completely.
While the cake is cooling, make the lemon glaze. In a small mixing bowl, whisk together the powdered sugar, lemon juice, and lemon zest until smooth.
Once the cake has cooled, spoon the lemon glaze over the top of the cake, spreading it out evenly with a spatula.
Let the glaze set for a few minutes before slicing and serving the cake. Enjoy!

Vanilla Ice Cream

Ingredients:

2 cans (14 oz each) full-fat coconut milk
1/2 cup granulated sugar
2 tbsp cornstarch
1 tbsp vanilla extract

Instructions:

In a medium saucepan, whisk together the coconut milk, sugar, and cornstarch until smooth.
Place the saucepan over medium heat, and cook the mixture, stirring constantly, until it thickens and comes to a simmer.
Reduce the heat to low, and continue to cook the mixture for an additional 2-3 minutes, or until it's thick enough to coat the back of a spoon.
Remove the saucepan from the heat, and stir in the vanilla extract.
Let the mixture cool to room temperature, then transfer it to an ice cream maker, and churn according to the manufacturer's instructions.
Once the ice cream is churned, transfer it to a freezer-safe container, and freeze for at least 2-3 hours, or until it's firm.
Remove the ice cream from the freezer, and let it sit at room temperature for a few minutes before scooping and serving. Enjoy!
Note: For a creamier texture, you can add 1/2 cup of vegan heavy cream (such as coconut cream) to the mixture before churning.

Vegan Fajitas

Ingredients:

1 red bell pepper, sliced
1 green bell pepper, sliced
1 yellow onion, sliced
1 tbsp olive oil
1 tsp ground cumin
1 tsp chili powder
1/2 tsp paprika
1/4 tsp garlic powder
1/4 tsp onion powder
Salt and pepper, to taste
4-6 tortillas (flour or corn)
Optional toppings: diced avocado, fresh cilantro, salsa, hot sauce, vegan sour cream

Instructions:

Heat a large skillet over medium heat. Add olive oil, bell peppers, and onion. Sauté for 5-7 minutes, or until the vegetables are tender.
In a small bowl, mix together the ground cumin, chili powder, paprika, garlic powder, onion powder, salt, and pepper.
Sprinkle the spice mixture over the vegetables, stirring well to coat. Cook for an additional 2-3 minutes, or until the spices are fragrant and the vegetables are evenly coated.
Warm up the tortillas in the oven, microwave, or on a dry skillet.
Assemble the fajitas by spooning the vegetable mixture onto the center of each tortilla. Add optional toppings such as diced avocado, fresh cilantro, salsa, hot sauce, and/or vegan sour cream, if desired.
Serve hot and enjoy your delicious vegan fajitas!

Banana Bread

Ingredients:

3 ripe bananas, mashed
1/4 cup vegan butter, melted
1/4 cup unsweetened applesauce
1/2 cup granulated sugar
1 teaspoon vanilla extract
1 1/2 cups all-purpose flour
1 teaspoon baking soda
1/2 teaspoon salt
1/2 teaspoon ground cinnamon
Optional add-ins: chopped nuts, chocolate chips, or dried fruit

Directions:

Preheat your oven to 350°F (175°C). Grease a 9x5 inch loaf pan or line it with parchment paper.
In a mixing bowl, combine the mashed bananas, melted vegan butter, applesauce, granulated sugar, and vanilla extract. Stir until well-combined.
In a separate mixing bowl, whisk together the flour, baking soda, salt, and ground cinnamon.
Gradually stir the dry ingredients into the wet mixture until just combined. If you're adding any optional add-ins, fold them in now.
Pour the batter into the prepared loaf pan.
Bake for 50-60 minutes or until a toothpick inserted into the center of the bread comes out clean.
Let the bread cool in the pan for 10-15 minutes before removing it from the pan and placing it on a wire rack to cool completely.
Slice and serve the vegan banana bread as desired. Enjoy!
Note: This recipe is easily customizable! Feel free to add in your favorite nuts, chocolate chips, or dried fruit to give it an extra burst of flavor.

Vegan Brownies

Ingredients:

1 cup all-purpose flour
1 cup granulated sugar
1/2 cup unsweetened cocoa powder
1 teaspoon baking powder
1/2 teaspoon salt
1/2 cup vegetable oil
1/2 cup unsweetened applesauce
1 teaspoon vanilla extract
1/2 cup vegan chocolate chips

Instructions:

Preheat the oven to 350°F (180°C) and line an 8x8 inch baking pan with parchment paper.
In a large mixing bowl, whisk together the flour, sugar, cocoa powder, baking powder, and salt.
Add the vegetable oil, applesauce, and vanilla extract to the dry ingredients and stir until well combined.
Fold in the vegan chocolate chips.
Pour the batter into the prepared baking pan and smooth the surface with a spatula.
Bake for 25-30 minutes, or until a toothpick inserted in the center comes out clean.
Let the brownies cool in the pan for 10 minutes, then transfer them to a wire rack to cool completely.
Once cooled, slice the brownies into desired serving size and enjoy!
These vegan brownies are rich, chocolatey, and indulgent. They're perfect for satisfying your sweet tooth without any animal products. Enjoy!

Margherita Pizza

Ingredients:

1 batch of pizza dough (store-bought or homemade)
1/2 cup tomato sauce
1/2 teaspoon dried oregano
1/4 teaspoon garlic powder
1/4 teaspoon salt
1/4 teaspoon black pepper
1/2 cup vegan mozzarella cheese, shredded
1 large tomato, thinly sliced
Fresh basil leaves, chopped

Instructions:

Preheat your oven to 425°F (220°C). If you have a pizza stone, place it in the oven while it preheats.
Roll out your pizza dough on a floured surface until it's about 1/4 inch thick. Transfer the dough to a piece of parchment paper.
In a small bowl, mix together the tomato sauce, oregano, garlic powder, salt, and black pepper. Spread the mixture over the pizza dough, leaving a small border around the edges.
Sprinkle the shredded vegan mozzarella cheese over the sauce.
Arrange the tomato slices on top of the cheese.
Transfer the pizza on the parchment paper to the preheated pizza stone or a baking sheet.
Bake the pizza for 10-12 minutes, or until the crust is golden brown and the cheese is melted and bubbly.
Remove the pizza from the oven and sprinkle with fresh chopped basil.
Slice and serve hot.
Enjoy your delicious and vegan-friendly margherita pizza!

Ginger Loaf Cake

Ingredients:

2 cups all-purpose flour
1 tsp baking powder
1 tsp baking soda
1/2 tsp salt
1 tbsp ground ginger
1 tsp ground cinnamon
1/4 tsp ground nutmeg
1/2 cup vegetable oil
1/2 cup molasses
1/2 cup brown sugar
1 cup unsweetened almond milk
1 tbsp apple cider vinegar

Instructions:

Preheat your oven to 350°F (175°C) and grease a 9x5 inch loaf pan.
In a large bowl, whisk together the flour, baking powder, baking soda, salt, ginger, cinnamon, and nutmeg until well combined.
In another bowl, whisk together the vegetable oil, molasses, brown sugar, almond milk, and apple cider vinegar until well combined.
Pour the wet ingredients into the dry ingredients and stir until just combined. Do not overmix.
Pour the batter into the prepared loaf pan and bake for 45-50 minutes, or until a toothpick inserted into the center of the cake comes out clean.
Let the cake cool in the pan for 10 minutes before transferring it to a wire rack to cool completely.
Serve the ginger loaf cake sliced and enjoy!
Optional: If you want to add some extra sweetness, you can make a simple glaze by whisking together 1 cup powdered sugar and 2-3 tbsp almond milk until smooth. Drizzle the glaze over the cooled cake before serving.
ChatGPT Feb 13 Version. Free Research Preview. Our goal is to make AI systems more natural and safe to interact with. Your feedback will help us improve.

Vegan Sausage Rolls

Ingredients:

For the filling:

1 can (15 oz/425 g) of chickpeas, drained and rinsed
1/2 cup (50 g) of rolled oats
1/4 cup (30 g) of nutritional yeast
1 tbsp (15 ml) of soy sauce
1 tsp (5 g) of smoked paprika
1 tsp (5 g) of garlic powder
1/2 tsp (2.5 g) of dried thyme
1/4 tsp (1.25 g) of cayenne pepper (optional)
Salt and pepper, to taste

For the pastry:

1 sheet of vegan puff pastry, thawed
1 tbsp (15 ml) of non-dairy milk

Instructions:

Preheat the oven to 375°F (190°C).

In a food processor, pulse the chickpeas, rolled oats, nutritional yeast, soy sauce, smoked paprika, garlic powder, thyme, cayenne pepper (if using), salt, and pepper until the mixture is smooth and forms a paste.
Roll out the puff pastry on a lightly floured surface into a large rectangle.
Cut the pastry in half lengthwise to create two long rectangles.
Divide the filling mixture in half, and roll each half into a log shape, placing it lengthwise on each rectangle of pastry.
Brush the edges of the pastry with non-dairy milk.
Roll the pastry up tightly around the filling, pressing the edges together to seal.
Cut the pastry rolls into smaller pieces, about 1-2 inches (2.5-5 cm) each.
Place the pastry rolls on a baking sheet lined with parchment paper.
Brush the tops of the pastry rolls with non-dairy milk.
Bake the vegan sausage rolls in the oven for 25-30 minutes, or until they are golden brown and crispy.
Serve hot, and enjoy your delicious vegan sausage rolls as a snack or appetizer!
These vegan sausage rolls are a great alternative to traditional sausage rolls, and they are easy to make and perfect for sharing. You can also customize the filling with your favorite spices and herbs.

Vegan Burritos

Ingredients:

1 cup (185 g) of uncooked brown rice
1 can (15 oz/425 g) of black beans, drained and rinsed
1 red bell pepper, diced
1/2 red onion, diced
1 avocado, diced
1 jalapeño pepper, diced (optional)
1 tbsp (15 ml) of olive oil
1 tsp (5 g) of ground cumin
1/2 tsp (2.5 g) of garlic powder
Salt and pepper, to taste
4-6 large flour tortillas
Vegan shredded cheese (such as cheddar or mozzarella) (optional)
Salsa, guacamole, or vegan sour cream, for serving (optional)

Instructions:

Cook the brown rice according to the package instructions.
In a mixing bowl, combine the black beans, red bell pepper, red onion, avocado, jalapeño pepper (if using), olive oil, cumin, garlic powder, salt, and pepper. Stir well to combine.
Heat a large skillet over medium heat. Add the black bean mixture to the skillet and cook for 5-7 minutes, stirring occasionally, until the vegetables are tender and the beans are heated through.
Warm the flour tortillas in the microwave or oven.
To assemble the vegan burritos, place a spoonful of brown rice in the center of each tortilla, followed by a spoonful of the black bean mixture. If using, sprinkle vegan shredded cheese on top.
Fold the sides of the tortilla over the filling, then roll it up tightly.
Repeat with the remaining tortillas and filling.
Serve the vegan burritos with salsa, guacamole, or vegan sour cream, if desired.
Enjoy your delicious and filling vegan burritos for lunch or dinner! You can also customize them by adding your favorite vegetables or toppings.

Vegan Quesadilla

Ingredients:

4 medium flour tortillas
1 can (15 oz/425 g) of black beans, drained and rinsed
1 red bell pepper, diced
1/2 red onion, diced
1 avocado, diced
1 jalapeño pepper, diced (optional)
1 tbsp (15 ml) of olive oil
1 tsp (5 g) of ground cumin
1/2 tsp (2.5 g) of garlic powder
Salt and pepper, to taste
Vegan shredded cheese (such as cheddar or mozzarella)

Instructions:

In a mixing bowl, combine the black beans, red bell pepper, red onion, avocado, jalapeño pepper (if using), olive oil, cumin, garlic powder, salt, and pepper. Stir well to combine.
Heat a large skillet over medium heat. Place one tortilla in the skillet and sprinkle with a thin layer of vegan shredded cheese. Spoon a quarter of the black bean mixture onto one half of the tortilla.
Fold the tortilla over the filling to create a half-moon shape. Press down lightly with a spatula to seal the edges.
Cook the vegan quesadilla for 2-3 minutes on each side until golden brown and crispy. Repeat with the remaining tortillas and black bean mixture.
Cut the vegan quesadillas into wedges and serve hot.
Enjoy your delicious and healthy vegan quesadillas for lunch or dinner! You can also serve them with salsa, guacamole, or vegan sour cream for added flavor.

Vegan Scrambled Eggs

Ingredients:

1 block (14 oz/400 g) of firm tofu, drained and crumbled
2 tbsp (30 ml) of olive oil
1/2 onion, diced
2 cloves of garlic, minced
1/2 red bell pepper, diced
1/2 yellow bell pepper, diced
1 tsp (5 g) of turmeric
1 tsp (5 ml) of soy sauce
Salt and pepper, to taste
Fresh parsley, chopped (optional)

Instructions:

Heat the olive oil in a non-stick skillet over medium heat. Add the onion and garlic, and sauté for 2-3 minutes until softened. Add the diced bell peppers to the skillet and cook for an additional 2-3 minutes until they are tender.
Add the crumbled tofu to the skillet and sprinkle with turmeric. Stir well to combine, and continue to cook for 5-7 minutes, stirring occasionally, until the tofu is lightly browned and crispy.
Add the soy sauce to the skillet and stir to combine. Season with salt and pepper to taste.
Continue to cook the tofu scramble for an additional 1-2 minutes until heated through.
Serve the vegan scrambled eggs hot, garnished with chopped parsley if desired.
Enjoy your delicious and healthy vegan scrambled eggs for breakfast or brunch!

Fluffy And Delicious Pancakes

Ingredients:

1 cup (120 g) of all-purpose flour
2 tbsp (25 g) of granulated sugar
2 tsp (10 g) of baking powder
1/2 tsp (2.5 g) of salt
1 cup (240 ml) of plant-based milk (such as almond or soy milk)
1 tbsp (15 ml) of apple cider vinegar
2 tbsp (30 ml) of vegetable oil
1 tsp (5 ml) of vanilla extract

Instructions:

In a mixing bowl, whisk together the flour, sugar, baking powder, and salt until well combined.
In a separate bowl, combine the plant-based milk and apple cider vinegar. Stir well and let sit for 2-3 minutes to curdle.
Add the vegetable oil and vanilla extract to the plant-based milk mixture and stir to combine.
Pour the wet ingredients into the dry ingredients and stir until just combined. Be careful not to overmix the batter, as this can make the pancakes tough.
Heat a non-stick pan or griddle over medium heat. Once hot, use a ladle or measuring cup to pour the pancake batter onto the pan. Cook for 2-3 minutes on each side, or until the pancakes are golden brown and cooked through.
Serve the vegan pancakes warm with your favorite toppings, such as fresh fruit, vegan butter, maple syrup, or vegan whipped cream.
Enjoy your delicious and fluffy vegan pancakes for breakfast or brunch!

Vegan Banana Fritters

Ingredients:

3 ripe bananas, mashed
1/2 cup (60 g) of all-purpose flour
1/4 cup (30 g) of cornstarch
1/4 cup (50 g) of granulated sugar
1 tsp (5 g) of baking powder
1/4 tsp (1.5 g) of salt
1/4 tsp (0.5 g) of ground cinnamon
1/4 cup (60 ml) of plant-based milk
Vegetable oil, for frying
Powdered sugar, for dusting

Instructions:

In a mixing bowl, combine the mashed bananas, flour, cornstarch, sugar, baking powder, salt, and cinnamon. Mix well until the batter is smooth.
Gradually add the plant-based milk to the batter, stirring until it is well incorporated and smooth.
Heat the vegetable oil in a deep frying pan over medium-high heat. The oil should be hot enough that a small drop of batter sizzles and floats to the surface immediately.
Use a spoon to drop the batter into the hot oil, making small fritters that are about 2-3 inches (5-7.5 cm) in diameter. Fry the fritters in batches, being careful not to overcrowd the pan.
Fry the fritters for about 2-3 minutes on each side, or until they are golden brown and crispy.
Use a slotted spoon to transfer the fritters to a paper towel-lined plate to drain any excess oil.
Repeat the frying process with the remaining batter until all the fritters are cooked.
Dust the crispy banana fritters with powdered sugar before serving.
Enjoy your crispy and sweet vegan banana fritters as a snack or dessert!

Pesto Pasta

Ingredients:

1 pound (450 g) of pasta (such as spaghetti or linguine)
2 cups (80 g) of fresh basil leaves, packed
1/2 cup (75 g) of pine nuts or walnuts
3 cloves of garlic, peeled
1/2 cup (120 ml) of olive oil
1/2 cup (40 g) of nutritional yeast
1 tsp (5 ml) of lemon juice
Salt and black pepper, to taste

Instructions:

Cook the pasta according to the package instructions. Drain and set aside.
While the pasta is cooking, prepare the pesto sauce. In a food processor or blender, combine the basil leaves, pine nuts or walnuts, and garlic. Pulse until everything is chopped.
With the food processor or blender running, slowly drizzle in the olive oil until the mixture becomes a smooth paste.
Add the nutritional yeast and lemon juice to the pesto sauce and pulse until everything is well combined.
Season the pesto sauce with salt and black pepper, to taste.
Toss the cooked pasta with the pesto sauce until everything is well coated.
Serve the vegan pesto pasta hot, with extra nutritional yeast and chopped fresh basil on top, if desired. Enjoy!

Vegan Ramen

Ingredients:

4 cups (960 ml) of vegetable broth
2 cloves of garlic, minced
1-inch (2.5 cm) piece of ginger, peeled and grated
1 tbsp (15 ml) of soy sauce or tamari
1 tbsp (15 ml) of miso paste
1 tsp (5 ml) of sesame oil
1/2 tsp (2.5 ml) of chili flakes (optional)
1 block of ramen noodles (or other noodles of your choice)
1 small carrot, julienned
1/2 cup (50 g) of sliced shiitake mushrooms
1/2 cup (50 g) of sliced green onions
1/2 cup (50 g) of chopped bok choy
1/2 cup (120 g) of firm tofu, cubed
Salt and black pepper, to taste

Instructions:

In a large pot, bring the vegetable broth, garlic, ginger, soy sauce or tamari, miso paste, sesame oil, and chili flakes (if using) to a boil over high heat.
Reduce the heat to low and let the broth simmer for 15-20 minutes.
While the broth is simmering, cook the ramen noodles according to the package instructions. Drain and set aside.
Add the julienned carrot, sliced shiitake mushrooms, chopped bok choy, and cubed tofu to the simmering broth. Let everything cook for another 5-7 minutes, or until the vegetables are tender.
To assemble the ramen bowls, divide the cooked noodles between 4 bowls. Pour the vegetable broth and vegetables over the noodles. Top each bowl with sliced green onions and black pepper, to taste.
Serve the vegan ramen immediately and enjoy!
Note: You can add any other vegetables or toppings that you like to your vegan ramen, such as sliced bell peppers, bean sprouts, nori seaweed, or pickled ginger.

Chocolate Cake

Ingredients:

1 and 3/4 cups all-purpose flour
1 and 3/4 cups granulated sugar
3/4 cup unsweetened cocoa powder
2 teaspoons baking soda
1 teaspoon baking powder
1 teaspoon salt
1 cup unsweetened almond milk
1/2 cup vegetable oil
2 teaspoons vanilla extract
1 cup boiling water

Instructions:

Preheat the oven to 350°F (175°C) and grease a 9x13 inch cake pan with non-stick spray.
In a large mixing bowl, whisk together the flour, sugar, cocoa powder, baking soda, baking powder, and salt until well combined.
In a separate mixing bowl, whisk together the almond milk, vegetable oil, and vanilla extract until smooth.
Add the wet ingredients to the dry ingredients and mix until just combined.
Pour the boiling water into the batter and mix until well combined.
Pour the batter into the prepared cake pan and smooth out the top with a spatula.
Bake for 35-40 minutes, or until a toothpick inserted into the center of the cake comes out clean.
Remove the cake from the oven and let it cool completely in the pan before slicing and serving.
Optional: Add a vegan chocolate frosting on top of the cake for extra richness and decadence.
Enjoy your delicious and moist vegan chocolate cake!

Chocolate Chip Cookies

Ingredients:

2 cups all-purpose flour
1 teaspoon baking powder
1/2 teaspoon baking soda
1/2 teaspoon salt
3/4 cup vegan butter, softened
3/4 cup brown sugar
1/2 cup granulated sugar
1/4 cup unsweetened applesauce
1 teaspoon vanilla extract
1 cup vegan chocolate chips

Instructions:

Preheat the oven to 350°F (175°C) and line a baking sheet with parchment paper.
In a medium mixing bowl, whisk together the flour, baking powder, baking soda, and salt until well combined.
In a separate mixing bowl, cream together the vegan butter, brown sugar, and granulated sugar until light and fluffy.
Add the applesauce and vanilla extract to the butter mixture and mix until well combined.
Add the dry ingredients to the wet ingredients and mix until just combined.
Fold in the vegan chocolate chips.
Roll the dough into 1-2 inch balls and place them on the prepared baking sheet, leaving about 2 inches of space between each cookie.
Bake for 10-12 minutes, or until the edges of the cookies are lightly golden brown.
Remove the baking sheet from the oven and let the cookies cool on the sheet for 5 minutes before transferring them to a wire rack to cool completely.
Enjoy your delicious and chewy vegan chocolate chip cookies!

Crispy Quinoa Cakes

Ingredients:

1 cup (180g) uncooked quinoa
2 cups (480 ml) water
1/2 cup (50 g) panko breadcrumbs (or other breadcrumbs of your choice)
1/2 cup (60 g) all-purpose flour
1/4 cup (30 g) nutritional yeast
1/4 cup (60 ml) olive oil
1/4 cup (60 ml) water
2 cloves of garlic, minced
1 small onion, chopped
1 tsp (5 ml) salt
1/2 tsp (2.5 ml) black pepper
1/4 tsp (1.25 ml) cayenne pepper (optional)
Vegetable oil for frying

Instructions:

Rinse the quinoa in a fine-mesh strainer and place it in a medium saucepan with 2 cups of water. Bring the water to a boil over high heat, then reduce the heat to low and simmer, covered, for 15-20 minutes or until the water has been absorbed and the quinoa is tender. Let the quinoa cool.

In a large mixing bowl, combine the cooled quinoa, panko breadcrumbs, all-purpose flour, nutritional yeast, garlic, onion, salt, black pepper, and cayenne pepper (if using). Mix everything together until well combined.
In a separate small bowl, whisk together the olive oil and 1/4 cup of water. Pour this mixture over the quinoa mixture and mix everything together until well combined.
Use your hands to form the quinoa mixture into 2-3 inch (5-7.5 cm) wide patties, about 1/2 inch (1.25 cm) thick.
Heat enough vegetable oil in a large frying pan over medium-high heat. Once the oil is hot, carefully place the quinoa cakes in the pan, making sure not to overcrowd them. Cook for 2-3 minutes on each side, or until golden brown and crispy.
Once cooked, place the quinoa cakes on a paper towel-lined plate to absorb any excess oil.
Serve the crispy quinoa cakes with a side salad or your favorite dipping sauce. Enjoy!
Note: These quinoa cakes can also be baked in the oven at 375°F (190°C) for 20-25 minutes, or until golden brown and crispy.

Vegan Lentil Meatballs

Ingredients:

1 cup (200 g) of dried brown lentils, rinsed and drained
2 cups (480 ml) of vegetable broth
1 small onion, chopped
3 cloves of garlic, minced
2 tbsp (30 ml) of olive oil
1/2 cup (60 g) of bread crumbs
1/4 cup (30 g) of nutritional yeast
1 tbsp (15 ml) of tomato paste
1 tbsp (15 ml) of soy sauce or tamari
1 tsp (5 ml) of dried oregano
1 tsp (5 ml) of dried basil
Salt and black pepper, to taste

Instructions:

In a medium saucepan, combine the rinsed lentils and vegetable broth. Bring the mixture to a boil over high heat, then reduce the heat to low and simmer, covered, for 25-30 minutes, or until the lentils are soft and most of the liquid has been absorbed. Drain off any excess liquid and let the lentils cool.
Preheat the oven to 400°F (200°C) and line a baking sheet with parchment paper. In a large skillet, heat the olive oil over medium heat. Add the chopped onion and sauté for 2-3 minutes, or until it's soft and translucent. Add the minced garlic and sauté for another 1-2 minutes.
In a large bowl, combine the cooked lentils, sautéed onion and garlic, bread crumbs, nutritional yeast, tomato paste, soy sauce or tamari, dried oregano, dried basil, salt, and black pepper. Mix everything together until well combined.
Using your hands, form the lentil mixture into golf ball-sized balls and place them on the prepared baking sheet. Bake the lentil meatballs for 20-25 minutes, or until they're golden brown and crispy on the outside.
Serve the vegan lentil meatballs with your favorite pasta or grain, and top with your favorite sauce. Enjoy!
Note: These lentil meatballs can also be frozen for later use. Simply place them on a baking sheet and freeze until solid, then transfer them to an airtight container or freezer bag. To reheat, simply bake them in a preheated oven at 400°F (200°C) for 10-15 minutes, or until heated through.

Falafel Burger

Ingredients:

1 can chickpeas, drained and rinsed
1/2 cup chopped onion
3 cloves garlic, minced
1/2 cup chopped fresh parsley
1/4 cup chopped fresh cilantro
1 tsp ground cumin
1 tsp ground coriander
1/2 tsp salt
1/4 tsp black pepper
1/4 cup all-purpose flour
1/4 cup breadcrumbs
4 vegan burger buns
Lettuce, sliced tomato, and sliced red onion for serving
Tahini sauce or vegan mayo for serving

Instructions:

Preheat your oven to 375°F.
In a food processor, pulse the chickpeas, onion, garlic, parsley, cilantro, cumin, coriander, salt, and black pepper until it forms a coarse mixture.
Transfer the mixture to a large mixing bowl and add the flour and breadcrumbs, then mix until everything is well combined.
Using your hands, form the mixture into four equal-sized patties.
Place the patties on a baking sheet lined with parchment paper and bake in the preheated oven for 20-25 minutes, or until golden brown and crispy.
Once the falafel burgers are cooked, remove them from the oven and let them cool for a few minutes.
While the burgers are cooling, lightly toast the burger buns and prepare any desired toppings.
Assemble the burgers by placing a falafel patty on the bottom half of each bun, then adding a layer of lettuce, tomato, and red onion on top.
Drizzle tahini sauce or vegan mayo over the toppings and add the top half of the bun.
Serve the burgers immediately and enjoy your delicious vegan falafel burgers!

Chickpea Curry

Ingredients:

1 tablespoon coconut oil
1 onion, chopped
3 cloves garlic, minced
1 tablespoon grated fresh ginger
1 tablespoon curry powder
1/2 teaspoon ground cumin
1/2 teaspoon ground coriander
1/4 teaspoon cayenne pepper
1 can (14 ounces) diced tomatoes, undrained
1 can (14 ounces) coconut milk
1 can (14 ounces) chickpeas, drained and rinsed
Salt and black pepper, to taste
Juice of 1/2 lemon
2 cups cooked rice, for serving
Chopped fresh cilantro, for garnish (optional)

Instructions:

Heat the coconut oil in a large saucepan or Dutch oven over medium heat. Add the onion, garlic, and ginger, and sauté until the onion is soft and translucent, about 5 minutes.
Add the curry powder, cumin, coriander, and cayenne pepper, and stir to coat the onion mixture. Cook for another 1-2 minutes, until the spices are fragrant.
Add the diced tomatoes and their juice, and stir to combine. Bring the mixture to a simmer, then reduce the heat to low and simmer for 10 minutes, stirring occasionally.
Add the coconut milk and chickpeas to the saucepan, and stir to combine. Simmer for another 10 minutes, until the chickpeas are tender and the sauce has thickened slightly.
Season the curry with salt and black pepper to taste, then stir in the lemon juice.
Serve the curry over cooked rice, and garnish with chopped cilantro if desired.
Enjoy your delicious vegan chickpea curry!

Vegan Alfredo Pasta

Ingredients:

12 oz (340 g) of fettuccine pasta
1 1/2 cups (360 ml) of unsweetened almond milk
1/2 cup (120 ml) of vegetable broth
1/2 cup (60 g) of nutritional yeast
3 cloves of garlic, minced
2 tbsp (30 ml) of olive oil
2 tbsp (30 ml) of cornstarch
1 tsp (5 ml) of salt
1/4 tsp (1.25 ml) of black pepper
Fresh parsley or basil, chopped, for garnish

Instructions:

Cook the fettuccine pasta according to the package instructions until al dente. Drain and set aside.
In a small bowl, whisk together the almond milk, vegetable broth, nutritional yeast, cornstarch, salt, and black pepper.
In a large skillet, heat the olive oil over medium heat. Add the minced garlic and sauté for 1-2 minutes, or until fragrant.
Pour the almond milk mixture into the skillet with the garlic and whisk continuously for 3-5 minutes, or until the sauce starts to thicken.
Add the cooked fettuccine to the skillet with the sauce and toss until the pasta is fully coated in the sauce.
Continue to cook the pasta and sauce for 2-3 minutes, or until the sauce has thickened and the pasta is heated through.
Divide the pasta alfredo into bowls and garnish with chopped fresh parsley or basil.
Enjoy your delicious vegan pasta alfredo!

Vegan Shepherds Pie

Ingredients:

For the filling:

1 tablespoon olive oil
1 large onion, chopped
2 garlic cloves, minced
2 medium carrots, peeled and chopped
2 celery stalks, chopped
1 cup sliced mushrooms
1 cup cooked lentils
1 cup vegetable broth
1 tablespoon tomato paste
1 tablespoon soy sauce or tamari
1 tablespoon flour
1/2 teaspoon dried thyme
Salt and pepper, to taste

For the mashed potato topping:

2 pounds potatoes, peeled and chopped
2 tablespoons vegan butter or olive oil
1/4 cup non-dairy milk
Salt and pepper, to taste

Instructions:

Preheat your oven to 375°F (190°C).

To make the filling, heat the olive oil in a large skillet over medium heat. Add the onion and garlic and sauté for 2-3 minutes until fragrant.
Add the chopped carrots, celery, and mushrooms and sauté for 5-7 minutes until the vegetables are tender.
Add the cooked lentils, vegetable broth, tomato paste, soy sauce or tamari, flour, dried thyme, salt, and pepper. Stir well to combine.
Bring the mixture to a simmer and cook for 5-7 minutes until the sauce has thickened.
Transfer the filling to a 9x13 inch baking dish.
To make the mashed potato topping, boil the potatoes in a large pot of salted water for 15-20 minutes until they are tender. Drain the potatoes and return them to the pot.
Add the vegan butter or olive oil, non-dairy milk, salt, and pepper to the pot with the potatoes. Mash the potatoes until they are smooth and creamy.
Spread the mashed potatoes over the top of the filling in the baking dish.
Bake the vegan shepherd's pie in the preheated oven for 25-30 minutes until the top is golden brown and crispy.
Serve hot and enjoy!
This vegan shepherd's pie is a comforting and satisfying meal that's perfect for chilly nights or for feeding a crowd. It's packed with plant-based protein and fiber, and it's also a great way to use up leftover mashed potatoes or cooked lentils.

Roasted Cauliflower

Roasted cauliflower is a simple and delicious side dish that's perfect for any meal. Here's a recipe that's easy to follow and yields a crispy and flavorful result:

Ingredients:

1 head of cauliflower, cut into bite-sized florets
3 tablespoons olive oil
1 teaspoon salt
1/2 teaspoon black pepper
1/2 teaspoon garlic powder
1/2 teaspoon paprika

Instructions:

Preheat your oven to 425°F (218°C) and line a baking sheet with parchment paper.
In a large mixing bowl, toss the cauliflower florets with olive oil, salt, pepper, garlic powder, and paprika until they are evenly coated.
Spread the cauliflower in a single layer on the prepared baking sheet, making sure not to overcrowd the pan. This will help the cauliflower to roast evenly and become crispy.
Place the baking sheet in the preheated oven and roast the cauliflower for 20-25 minutes or until it is golden brown and crispy on the outside.
Use a spatula to flip the cauliflower halfway through the cooking time to ensure even roasting.
Once the cauliflower is cooked to your desired level of crispiness, remove it from the oven and transfer it to a serving dish.
Garnish with fresh parsley or your favorite herbs, and serve hot.
Enjoy your delicious roasted cauliflower as a side dish or snack. It pairs well with grilled meats, roasted chicken, or can be enjoyed on its own as a healthy and flavorful snack.

Vegan Baked Oats

Ingredients:

2 cups rolled oats
2 cups unsweetened almond milk
2 ripe bananas, mashed
1/4 cup pure maple syrup
1 tsp vanilla extract
1 tsp ground cinnamon
1/2 tsp baking powder
Pinch of salt
1/2 cup chopped nuts (optional)

Instructions:

Preheat your oven to 375°F (190°C).
In a large mixing bowl, combine the rolled oats, almond milk, mashed bananas, maple syrup, vanilla extract, cinnamon, baking powder, and salt. Mix well until everything is fully combined.
Pour the mixture into a baking dish or a cast-iron skillet. Sprinkle the chopped nuts on top, if using.
Bake for 30-35 minutes or until the oats are golden brown and crispy on top.
Serve warm and enjoy!
Note: You can also add other toppings like fresh fruit, coconut flakes, or nut butter to make it more delicious.

Vegetable Biryani

For the biryani:

2 tablespoons of vegetable oil
1 onion, chopped
1 teaspoon of ginger paste
1 teaspoon of garlic paste
1 teaspoon of cumin seeds
1 teaspoon of coriander powder
1 teaspoon of garam masala
1/2 teaspoon of turmeric powder
1/2 teaspoon of red chili powder (optional)
2 cups of mixed vegetables (such as carrots, peas, potatoes, and green beans)
Salt to taste
1/4 cup of chopped fresh cilantro
1/4 cup of chopped fresh mint
1/2 cup of toasted cashews (optional)

Ingredients:

For the rice:

2 cups of basmati rice
4 cups of water
1 cinnamon stick
3-4 green cardamom pods
3-4 cloves
1 bay leaf
Salt to taste

Instructions:

Rinse the basmati rice in cold water until the water runs clear. Soak the rice in water for 20 minutes.
In a large pot, bring the 4 cups of water to a boil. Add the soaked rice, cinnamon stick, green cardamom pods, cloves, bay leaf, and salt to the pot. Stir well to combine.
Reduce the heat to low, cover the pot with a lid, and let the rice cook for 15-20 minutes, or until all the water has been absorbed and the rice is fully cooked.
Once the rice is cooked, remove the whole spices and fluff the rice with a fork. Set the rice aside.
In a large skillet, heat the vegetable oil over medium-high heat. Add the chopped onion and sauté for 2-3 minutes or until the onion is translucent.
Add the ginger paste, garlic paste, and cumin seeds to the skillet. Cook for 1-2 minutes, stirring constantly.
Add the coriander powder, garam masala, turmeric powder, and red chili powder (if using) to the skillet. Stir well to combine.
Add the mixed vegetables to the skillet and cook for 5-7 minutes or until the vegetables are tender. Season the vegetable mixture with salt to taste.
In a large bowl, combine the cooked rice, vegetable mixture, chopped fresh cilantro, chopped fresh mint, and toasted cashews (if using). Stir well to combine.
Transfer the biryani mixture to a serving dish and garnish with additional cilantro and mint. Serve hot and enjoy your delicious vegetable biryani!

Bolognese Pasta

Ingredients:

1 pound of spaghetti or pasta of your choice
1 large onion, chopped
3 garlic cloves, minced
2 carrots, finely chopped
2 celery stalks, finely chopped
1 red bell pepper, chopped
1 can (28 ounces) of crushed tomatoes
1 can (15 ounces) of tomato sauce
1 tablespoon of tomato paste
1 teaspoon of dried oregano
1 teaspoon of dried basil
1 teaspoon of dried thyme
1 teaspoon of salt
1/2 teaspoon of black pepper
2 tablespoons of olive oil
1/4 cup of chopped fresh parsley
Vegan Parmesan cheese for serving (optional)

Instructions:

Cook the pasta according to package instructions until al dente. Drain the pasta and set it aside.
In a large pot or Dutch oven, heat the olive oil over medium-high heat. Add the onion and sauté for 3-4 minutes, or until the onion is translucent.
Add the garlic, carrots, celery, and red bell pepper to the pot. Cook for 5-7 minutes or until the vegetables are tender.
Add the crushed tomatoes, tomato sauce, tomato paste, dried oregano, dried basil, dried thyme, salt, and black peper to the pot. Stir well to combine.
Bring the sauce to a boil, then reduce the heat to low and let it simmer for 20-25 minutes, stirring occasionally.
Once the sauce has thickened and the vegetables are tender, add the chopped fresh parsley and stir well.
Serve the sauce over the cooked pasta and top with vegan Parmesan cheese (if using). Enjoy your delicious vegan bolognese pasta!

Vegan Mac And Cheese

Ingredients:

1 pound elbow macaroni
1/4 cup vegan butter
1/4 cup all-purpose flour
3 cups unsweetened almond milk
1/4 cup nutritional yeast
1 tsp garlic powder
1 tsp onion powder
1 tsp ground mustard
Salt and pepper to taste

Instructions:

Cook the macaroni according to package directions until it is al dente.
While the macaroni is cooking, make the cheese sauce. In a medium saucepan, melt the vegan butter over medium heat.
Add the flour to the melted butter and whisk continuously until it forms a paste.
Gradually pour in the almond milk, whisking constantly, until the mixture is smooth.
Add the nutritional yeast, garlic powder, onion powder, ground mustard, salt, and pepper to the saucepan. Whisk until everything is fully combined.
Simmer the sauce over medium heat for 5-10 minutes or until it thickens.
Drain the cooked macaroni and add it to the cheese sauce. Mix well until the macaroni is fully coated in the sauce.
Serve immediately and enjoy!
Note: You can also bake the mac and cheese in the oven for an extra crispy top. Simply transfer the mixture to a baking dish, sprinkle with breadcrumbs or vegan cheese, and bake at 350°F (180°C) for 10-15 minutes or until golden brown.

Chocolate Ice Cream

Ingredients:

2 ripe bananas, peeled and sliced
1/2 cup unsweetened cocoa powder
1/2 cup pure maple syrup
1 can full-fat coconut milk
1 tsp pure vanilla extract

Instructions:

Add the sliced bananas to a blender or food processor and blend until smooth.
Add the cocoa powder, maple syrup, coconut milk, and vanilla extract to the blender and blend until well combined.
Transfer the mixture to an ice cream maker and churn according to the manufacturer's instructions, typically 20-25 minutes.
Transfer the ice cream to a container and freeze for at least 2 hours, or until firm.
When ready to serve, let the ice cream sit at room temperature for a few minutes to soften, then scoop and enjoy!
Note: If you don't have an ice cream \maker, you can still make this recipe by blending the ingredients and freezing them in an airtight container, stirring every 30 minutes until firm. It won't be as creamy as ice cream churned in a machine, but it will still be delicious!

Tomato Soup

Ingredients:

2 tablespoons olive oil
1 large onion, chopped
3 garlic cloves, minced
2 cans of whole peeled tomatoes
2 cups of vegetable broth
1/4 cup of fresh basil leaves, chopped
1/2 cup of heavy cream (optional)
Salt and pepper to taste
Croutons or bread for serving (optional)

Instructions:

In a large pot or Dutch oven, heat the olive oil over medium heat.
Add the onion and garlic and cook for 5-7 minutes until softened and translucent.
Add the cans of whole peeled tomatoes (with their juice) and stir to combine.
Add the vegetable broth and bring the mixture to a simmer.
Cook for 15-20 minutes until the tomatoes have broken down and the flavors have melded together.
Add the chopped basil leaves and stir to combine.
Using an immersion blender or working in batches with a regular blender, puree the soup until smooth.
Return the soup to the pot and add the heavy cream (if using). Stir to combine.
Season with salt and pepper to taste.
Serve the soup hot with croutons or bread for dipping, if desired.
Enjoy your tomato basil soup! It's a comforting and classic dish that's perfect for any time of year.

Delicious Broccoli Soup

Ingredients:

1 head of broccoli, chopped into florets
1 onion, chopped
2 cloves of garlic, minced
1 tablespoon olive oil
4 cups vegetable broth
1/2 teaspoon ground cumin
1/4 teaspoon ground turmeric
Salt and pepper to taste
1/2 cup coconut milk
2 tablespoons nutritional yeast (optional)

Instructions:

In a large pot, heat the olive oil over medium heat.
Add the chopped onion and minced garlic to the pot and sauté until soft and translucent.
Add the chopped broccoli to the pot and stir well to combine with the onions and garlic.
Add the vegetable broth, ground cumin, ground turmeric, salt, and pepper to the pot and bring to a boil.
Reduce the heat to low and let the soup simmer for about 20 minutes, or until the broccoli is tender.
Use an immersion blender or transfer the soup to a blender and blend until smooth and creamy.
Stir in the coconut milk and nutritional yeast (if using).
Adjust the seasoning to taste, adding more salt, pepper, cumin, or turmeric as needed.
Serve hot with crusty bread or crackers on top, and enjoy!

Noodles With Cashew Coconut Sauce

Ingredients:

8 oz. of noodles (your choice of pasta, rice noodles, or soba noodles)
1/2 cup raw cashews
1/2 cup coconut milk
2 tablespoons soy sauce
2 tablespoons rice vinegar
2 tablespoons maple syrup
1 tablespoon sriracha (optional)
1 tablespoon grated ginger
2 garlic cloves, minced
2 green onions, sliced (optional)
2 tablespoons chopped cilantro (optional)
1 tablespoon coconut oil or vegetable oil

Instructions:

Cook noodles according to package instructions until al dente. Drain and set aside.
In a blender or food processor, blend the cashews, coconut milk, soy sauce, rice vinegar, maple syrup, sriracha, ginger, and garlic until smooth and creamy.
In a large skillet or wok, heat the coconut oil over medium heat.
Add the cashew coconut sauce to the skillet and cook for 2-3 minutes, stirring constantly.
Add the cooked noodles to the skillet and toss to coat in the sauce.
Cook for an additional 2-3 minutes until the noodles are heated through.
Garnish with sliced green onions and chopped cilantro (if using).
Serve hot and enjoy!
This noodles with cashew coconut sauce recipe is a vegan, gluten-free, and dairy-free alternative to traditional pasta dishes. The cashew coconut sauce adds a creamy and nutty flavor that complements the noodles perfectly. You can also add your favorite veggies like broccoli, bell peppers, or snap peas to make it more colorful and nutritious.

Maki Sushi

Ingredients:

2 cups sushi rice
2 1/2 cups water
1/4 cup rice vinegar
1 tablespoon sugar
1 teaspoon salt
4 sheets of nori seaweed
1/2 cup thinly sliced carrots
1/2 cup thinly sliced cucumber
1/2 cup thinly sliced avocado
1/2 cup thinly sliced red bell pepper
1/4 cup sliced scallions
Soy sauce, wasabi, and pickled ginger for serving

Instructions:

Rinse the sushi rice in cold water until the water runs clear.
In a medium saucepan, combine the rinsed rice and water. Bring to a boil, then reduce the heat to low, cover, and simmer for 18-20 minutes or until the rice is tender and the water has been absorbed.
In a small bowl, whisk together the rice vinegar, sugar, and salt until the sugar and salt have dissolved.
Once the rice is cooked, transfer it to a large bowl and add the rice vinegar mixture. Stir gently to combine.
Lay a sheet of nori seaweed on a clean surface, shiny side down.
Wet your hands with water and take a small amount of rice, about the size of a golf ball, and spread it evenly over the nori, leaving a 1-inch border at the top edge.
Add a few slices of carrots, cucumber, avocado, red bell pepper, and scallions to the center of the rice.
Using the border of rice at the top edge as a guide, roll the sushi tightly.
Repeat with the remaining ingredients.
Slice the sushi rolls into bite-size pieces.
Serve with soy sauce, wasabi, and pickled ginger.

This vegan maki sushi is a healthy and delicious meal that's perfect for a light lunch or dinner. The combination of fresh vegetables and creamy avocado makes for a satisfying and flavorful bite. You can customize the recipe by using your favorite vegetables or adding a protein such as tofu or tempeh.

Easy Vegan Noodle

Ingredients:

8 oz of noodles of your choice (such as spaghetti or udon)
1/2 cup chopped mushrooms
1/2 cup chopped carrots
1/2 cup chopped red bell pepper
1/2 cup chopped green onions
2 cloves garlic, minced
1/4 cup soy sauce
1 tablespoon sesame oil
1 tablespoon rice vinegar
1 tablespoon maple syrup
1 teaspoon ginger paste
1 teaspoon cornstarch
Salt and black pepper, to taste

Instructions:

Cook the noodles according to the package instructions. Drain and set aside.
In a small bowl, whisk together the soy sauce, sesame oil, rice vinegar, maple syrup, ginger paste, cornstarch, salt, and pepper.
In a large skillet, heat some oil over medium-high heat. Add the chopped mushrooms, carrots, and red bell pepper. Cook for 5-7 minutes or until the vegetables are tender.
Add the minced garlic and cook for an additional minute, stirring constantly.
Add the chopped green onions and the soy sauce mixture to the skillet. Cook for 2-3 minutes or until the sauce thickens.
Add the cooked noodles to the skillet and toss to coat with the sauce.
Serve hot and enjoy!

This vegan noodle dish is quick and easy to make, and it's packed with flavor and nutrients. You can customize the recipe by using your favorite type of noodles and vegetables. It's a great option for a weeknight dinner or a quick lunch.

Mediterranean Stuffed Eggplant

Here's a recipe for a delicious Mediterranean stuffed eggplant:

Ingredients:

2 medium eggplants
1/2 cup uncooked quinoa
1 can chickpeas, drained and rinsed
1/2 cup chopped cherry tomatoes
1/4 cup chopped fresh parsley
1/4 cup chopped fresh mint
1/4 cup chopped Kalamata olives
1/4 cup crumbled feta cheese
1 tablespoon olive oil
2 cloves garlic, minced
Salt and black pepper, to taste

Instructions:

Preheat oven to 400°F (200°C).
Cut the eggplants in half lengthwise and scoop out the flesh, leaving about 1/2 inch around the edges. Reserve the scooped-out flesh for later.
Place the eggplant halves on a baking sheet lined with parchment paper, drizzle with olive oil, and sprinkle with salt and pepper. Roast for 20-25 minutes or until they are tender and golden brown.
While the eggplants are roasting, cook the quinoa according to package instructions.
In a large mixing bowl, combine the cooked quinoa, chickpeas, chopped cherry tomatoes, chopped parsley, chopped mint, chopped Kalamata olives, crumbled feta cheese, minced garlic, and the reserved eggplant flesh. Mix well.
Remove the roasted eggplants from the oven and stuff each half with the quinoa mixture.
Return the stuffed eggplants to the oven and bake for an additional 10-15 minutes, or until the filling is heated through and the feta cheese is melted and slightly golden.
Serve hot and enjoy!

This Mediterranean stuffed eggplant is a tasty and healthy meal that's perfect for vegetarians and meat-eaters alike. It's packed with flavor and nutrients, and it's sure to become a family favorite!

Vegan Waffles

Ingredients:

2 cups all-purpose flour
2 tablespoons granulated sugar
1 tablespoon baking powder
1/2 teaspoon salt
1 3/4 cups unsweetened almond milk (or any plant-based milk)
1/2 cup vegetable oil
1 teaspoon vanilla extract

Instructions:
In a large mixing bowl, whisk together the flour, sugar, baking powder, and salt until combined.
In a separate bowl, whisk together the almond milk, vegetable oil, and vanilla extract.
Add the wet ingredients to the dry ingredients and stir until just combined. Be careful not to overmix, as this can lead to tough waffles.
Heat a waffle iron according to its instructions. Once it's hot, spray it with non-stick cooking spray.
Scoop the batter onto the waffle iron using a 1/4 cup measure or a ladle, spreading it out evenly. Close the lid and cook for 3-5 minutes, or until the waffles are golden brown and crispy.
Serve the waffles immediately with your favorite toppings, such as fresh fruit, vegan whipped cream, or maple syrup.
Enjoy your delicious vegan waffles!

Vegan French Toast

Ingredients:

1 loaf of bread, sliced
1 cup of plant-based milk (such as almond milk, soy milk, or oat milk)
1 tablespoon of ground flaxseed
1 teaspoon of vanilla extract
1 teaspoon of ground cinnamon
1/4 teaspoon of ground nutmeg
1 tablespoon of maple syrup
1 tablespoon of vegetable oil
Toppings (optional): fresh fruit, vegan whipped cream, or maple syrup

Instructions:

In a shallow bowl, whisk together the plant-based milk, ground flaxseed, vanilla extract, ground cinnamon, ground nutmeg, and maple syrup.
Heat a non-stick pan over medium heat and add the vegetable oil.
Dip each slice of bread into the milk mixture, ensuring that both sides are coated evenly.
Place the bread in the pan and cook for 2-3 minutes on each side, or until the French toast is golden brown.
Remove the French toast from the pan and transfer to a plate.
Repeat with the remaining slices of bread, adding more oil to the pan as needed.
Serve the French toast immediately with your favorite toppings, such as fresh fruit, vegan whipped cream, or maple syrup.
Enjoy your delicious vegan French toast!

Sweet Potato Salad

Ingredients:

2 large sweet potatoes, peeled and cubed
1/2 red onion, diced
1 red bell pepper, diced
1/4 cup chopped fresh cilantro
1/4 cup chopped pecans
2 tablespoons olive oil
2 tablespoons apple cider vinegar
1 tablespoon honey
1 teaspoon Dijon mustard
Salt and black pepper, to taste

Instructions:

Preheat oven to 400°F (200°C).
Spread the sweet potato cubes in a single layer on a baking sheet lined with parchment paper. Drizzle with 1 tablespoon of olive oil and sprinkle with salt and pepper. Toss to coat.
Roast sweet potatoes for 25-30 minutes or until they are tender and golden brown. Remove from the oven and let cool.
In a small bowl, whisk together 1 tablespoon of olive oil, apple cider vinegar, honey, Dijon mustard, salt, and pepper until well combined.
In a large mixing bowl, combine the cooled sweet potatoes, diced red onion, diced red bell pepper, chopped cilantro, and chopped pecans.
Pour the dressing over the sweet potato mixture and toss to coat.
Serve chilled or at room temperature.

This sweet potato salad is perfect for a healthy and flavorful side dish for any meal. Enjoy!

Chickpea Salald Sandwich

Ingredients:

1 can chickpeas, drained and rinsed
1/4 cup diced red onion
1/4 cup diced celery
2 tbsp chopped fresh parsley
2 tbsp chopped fresh dill
2 tbsp vegan mayo
1 tbsp dijon mustard
1 tbsp fresh lemon juice
Salt and pepper, to taste
Sliced bread or buns of your choice
Lettuce, tomato, or any additional toppings you prefer

Instructions:

Preheat oven to 375°F (190°C).
In a bowl, mash the chickpeas with a fork or potato masher until they're mostly broken up.
Add in the red onion, celery, parsley, and dill, and stir until combined.
In a separate small bowl, mix together the vegan mayo, dijon mustard, lemon juice, salt, and pepper.
Pour the mayo mixture over the chickpea mixture and stir until everything is well-coated.
Line a baking sheet with parchment paper.
Scoop the chickpea salad onto the baking sheet using a spoon or cookie scoop, forming each scoop into a round patty shape.
Bake the chickpea patties for 15-20 minutes, until they're crispy on the outside and warmed through.
Toast your bread or buns, and assemble your sandwich with the chickpea patties, lettuce, tomato, and any other toppings you like.
Enjoy your delicious and protein-packed chickpea salad sandwich!

Carrot Cake

Ingredients:

2 cups all-purpose flour
2 tsp baking powder
1 tsp baking soda
1 tsp cinnamon
1/2 tsp nutmeg
1/2 tsp salt
1/2 cup vegetable oil
1/2 cup unsweetened applesauce
1 cup granulated sugar
1/4 cup unsweetened almond milk
2 tsp vanilla extract
2 cups grated carrots
1/2 cup chopped walnuts (optional)
Vegan cream cheese frosting
(recipe below)

Instructions:

Preheat your oven to 350°F (180°C). Grease a 9-inch cake pan with cooking spray.
In a medium bowl, whisk together the flour, baking powder, baking soda, cinnamon, nutmeg, and salt until well combined.
In a large bowl, whisk together the vegetable oil, applesauce, sugar, almond milk, and vanilla extract until smooth.
Add the dry ingredients to the wet ingredients, stirring until just combined.
Fold in the grated carrots and chopped walnuts (if using) until evenly distributed.
Pour the batter into the prepared cake pan and bake for 35-40 minutes, or until a toothpick inserted into the center of the cake comes out clean.
Let the cake cool in the pan for 5-10 minutes before transferring it to a wire rack to cool completely.
Once the cake has cooled, spread the vegan cream cheese frosting on top and decorate with additional chopped walnuts, if desired.

Vegan Cream Cheese Frosting:
1/2 cup vegan butter, softened
1/2 cup vegan cream cheese, softened
2 cups powdered sugar
1 tsp vanilla extract
Instructions:
In a large bowl, cream together the vegan butter and cream cheese until light and fluffy.
Add the powdered sugar and vanilla extract, and beat until smooth.
If the frosting is too thick, add a splash of almond milk to thin it out.
Spread the frosting on top of the cooled carrot cake and enjoy!

Kidney Bean Curry

Ingredients:

1 tablespoon vegetable oil
1 large onion, chopped
4 garlic cloves, minced
1 tablespoon grated fresh ginger
1 tablespoon curry powder
1 teaspoon ground cumin
1/2 teaspoon ground coriander
1/4 teaspoon cayenne pepper
1 can (14.5 oz) diced tomatoes, undrained
2 cans (15 oz each) kidney beans, drained and rinsed
1/2 teaspoon salt
1/4 teaspoon black pepper
1/4 cup chopped fresh cilantro
Cooked rice, for serving

Instructions:

In a large skillet, heat the oil over medium heat. Add the onion and cook, stirring occasionally, until softened, about 5 minutes.
Add the garlic and ginger and cook for 1-2 minutes, stirring constantly.
Add the curry powder, cumin, coriander, and cayenne pepper and cook for 1-2 minutes, stirring constantly, until fragrant.
Add the diced tomatoes (with their juices), kidney beans, salt, and black pepper. Bring to a simmer and cook for 10-15 minutes, stirring occasionally, until the sauce has thickened and the beans are heated through.
Stir in the cilantro and remove from the heat.
Serve the curry over cooked rice.
Enjoy your vegan kidney bean curry!

Crispy Baked Falafel

Here's a recipe for crispy baked falafel:

Ingredients:

2 cups cooked chickpeas, drained and rinsed
1/2 onion, chopped
3 cloves garlic, minced
1/4 cup chopped fresh parsley
1/4 cup chopped fresh cilantro
1 teaspoon ground cumin
1 teaspoon ground coriander
1/2 teaspoon paprika
1/4 teaspoon cayenne pepper
1 teaspoon salt
1/4 teaspoon black pepper
1/4 cup all-purpose flour
1 teaspoon baking powder
2 tablespoons olive oil

Instructions:

Preheat the oven to 375°F (190°C) and line a baking sheet with parchment paper.
In a food processor, pulse the chickpeas, onion, garlic, parsley, cilantro, cumin, coriander, paprika, cayenne pepper, salt, and black pepper until the mixture is coarse and crumbly.
Add the flour and baking powder to the food processor and pulse until the mixture forms a dough.
Form the dough into 2-inch balls and flatten slightly to form patties.
Place the patties on the prepared baking sheet and brush each one with olive oil.
Bake for 20-25 minutes, or until the falafel is crispy and golden brown.
Serve the falafel with pita bread, hummus, and your favorite veggies. Enjoy!

Macro Veggie Bowl

Ingredients:

1 cup quinoa
1 sweet potato, cubed
1 red bell pepper, sliced
1 yellow bell pepper, sliced
1 zucchini, sliced
1 cup broccoli florets
1 avocado, sliced
1/4 cup pumpkin seeds
1/4 cup sunflower seeds
1/4 cup chopped fresh parsley
Salt and pepper, to taste
Olive oil, for roasting

For the dressing:

1/4 cup tahini
1/4 cup apple cider vinegar
2 tablespoons honey
1 tablespoon dijon mustard
Juice of 1 lemon
Salt and pepper, to taste
Water, as needed to thin the dressing

Instructions:

Preheat the oven to 400°F. Line a baking sheet with parchment paper.
Cook quinoa according to package instructions.
Place sweet potato, red bell pepper, yellow bell pepper, zucchini, and broccoli on the baking sheet. Drizzle with olive oil and season with salt and pepper.
Roast in the oven for 20-25 minutes or until vegetables are tender and lightly browned.
In a small bowl, whisk together tahini, apple cider vinegar, honey, dijon mustard, lemon juice, salt, and pepper. Add water to thin the dressing if needed.
To assemble the bowl, divide cooked quinoa among serving bowls. Top with roasted vegetables, sliced avocado, pumpkin seeds, sunflower seeds, and chopped parsley. Drizzle with the dressing and serve. Enjoy your macro veggie bowl!

Easy Vegan Parmesan Cheese

Ingredients:

1 cup raw cashews
1/4 cup nutritional yeast
1 tsp garlic powder
1 tsp onion powder
1/2 tsp salt

Instructions:

Add the raw cashews to a food processor and pulse until they're finely ground, but not turned into cashew butter.
Add the nutritional yeast, garlic powder, onion powder, and salt to the food processor and pulse until everything is well combined and has a fine texture.
Taste the mixture and adjust the seasonings as necessary.
Transfer the vegan parmesan cheese to an airtight container and store it in the refrigerator until ready to use.

To use the vegan parmesan cheese, sprinkle it over pasta, salads, roasted vegetables, or any other dish where you'd normally use parmesan cheese. It adds a nutty, savory flavor that's sure to please vegans and non-vegans alike.

Mushroom Burger

Here's a recipe for a delicious mushroom burger:

Ingredients:

4 portobello mushroom caps
1/4 cup balsamic vinegar
2 tablespoons olive oil
1 teaspoon dried thyme
1/2 teaspoon garlic powder
Salt and black pepper
4 burger buns
Toppings of your choice
(lettuce, tomato, onion, etc.)

Instructions:

Preheat your grill or grill pan to medium-high heat.
Clean the portobello mushrooms and remove the stems. Use a spoon to gently scrape out the gills and discard them.
In a small bowl, whisk together the balsamic vinegar, olive oil, thyme, garlic powder, salt, and pepper.
Brush the marinade over both sides of the mushroom caps, making sure they are fully coated.
Place the mushrooms on the grill and cook for 4-5 minutes on each side, or until they are tender and juicy.
While the mushrooms are cooking, toast your burger buns on the grill.
Assemble your burgers by placing the cooked mushrooms on the toasted buns and adding your desired toppings.
Serve immediately and enjoy your delicious mushroom burger!

Cauliflower Rice

Here's how to make cauliflower rice:

Ingredients:

1 head of cauliflower
1 tablespoon olive oil
Salt and pepper to taste

- Instructions:
-
- Wash and dry the cauliflower head.
- Cut off the florets from the stem and discard the stem.
- Place the cauliflower florets in a food processor and pulse until they resemble rice.
- Heat the olive oil in a large skillet over medium-high heat.
- Add the cauliflower rice to the skillet and stir to combine with the oil.
- Season with salt and pepper to taste.
- Cook for 5-7 minutes, stirring occasionally, until the cauliflower rice is tender and slightly golden brown.
- Remove from heat and use as a base for your grain-free grain bowl.

Roasted Veggie Grain Bowl

Ingredients:

1 small sweet potato, peeled and cubed
1 small head of broccoli, chopped into florets
1 small red onion, diced
1 red bell pepper, diced
2 tablespoons olive oil
1 teaspoon salt
1 teaspoon black pepper
1 cup quinoa, rinsed and drained
2 cups vegetable broth or water
1/4 cup pepitas (pumpkin seeds)

For the Kale Pesto:

2 cups packed kale leaves, stems removed
1/2 cup walnuts
1/4 cup nutritional yeast
3 garlic cloves
1/2 cup olive oil
1/2 teaspoon salt
1/2 teaspoon black pepper

Instructions:
Preheat the oven to 400°F (200°C).
In a large bowl, combine the sweet potato, broccoli, red onion, red bell pepper, olive oil, salt, and black pepper. Toss to coat the vegetables evenly.
Spread the vegetables out in a single layer on a baking sheet. Roast for 20-25 minutes, or until the vegetables are tender and browned in spots.
While the vegetables are roasting, prepare the quinoa. In a medium saucepan, bring the quinoa and vegetable broth or water to a boil over high heat. Reduce the heat to low, cover the saucepan, and simmer for 15-20 minutes, or until the liquid is absorbed and the quinoa is tender.
In a small dry skillet, toast the pepitas over medium heat for 2-3 minutes, or until they are lightly browned and fragrant.
To make the kale pesto, combine the kale leaves, walnuts, nutritional yeast, garlic, olive oil, salt, and black pepper in a food processor. Pulse until the mixture is smooth and creamy.
To assemble the bowls, divide the cooked quinoa and roasted vegetables among four bowls. Drizzle each bowl with some of the kale pesto and sprinkle with toasted pepitas.
Serve immediately and enjoy!

Vegan Cream Cheese

Ingredients:

1 cup raw cashews, soaked overnight in water or boiled for 10 minutes
1/4 cup unsweetened non-dairy yogurt
2 tbsp lemon juice
1 tbsp apple cider vinegar
1/2 tsp salt
1-2 tbsp non-dairy milk, as needed to achieve desired consistency

Instructions:

Drain and rinse the soaked cashews and add them to a food processor.
Add the non-dairy yogurt, lemon juice, apple cider vinegar, and salt to the food processor and blend everything together until smooth and creamy.
If the mixture is too thick, add a tablespoon or two of non-dairy milk to thin it out to your desired consistency.
Taste the vegan cream cheese and adjust the seasoning as needed, adding more salt or lemon juice if desired.
Transfer the vegan cream cheese to an airtight container and store it in the refrigerator until ready to use.
This vegan cream cheese is perfect for spreading on bagels or toast, using as a dip for veggies or crackers, or as a creamy filling in wraps or sandwiches. It's a healthy and delicious alternative to traditional cream cheese that's dairy-free and packed with plant-based protein and healthy fats.

Delicious Rice Bliss Bowl

Here's how you can prepare a delicious rice bliss bowl:

Ingredients:

1 cup brown rice
2 cups water
1 block of tempeh, sliced
1 tablespoon soy sauce
1 tablespoon sesame oil
1/2 teaspoon garlic powder
1/2 teaspoon onion powder
1/2 teaspoon smoked paprika
1/2 cup kimchi
1/2 cup shredded carrots
1/2 cup shredded red cabbage
1/4 cup roasted peanuts, chopped
Fresh cilantro for garnish

For the peanut sauce:

1/4 cup natural peanut butter
2 tablespoons soy sauce
1 tablespoon maple syrup
1 tablespoon rice vinegar
1/2 teaspoon sesame oil
1/2 teaspoon sriracha sauce (optional)
Water to thin as needed

Instructions:

Rinse the brown rice and place it in a medium-sized pot with 2 cups of water. Bring it to a boil over high heat, then lower the heat and let it simmer for 35-40 minutes, or until the rice is tender and cooked through.
In the meantime, preheat a grill or grill pan over medium-high heat. In a small bowl, mix together soy sauce, sesame oil, garlic powder, onion powder, and smoked paprika. Brush the tempeh slices with the mixture and place them on the grill. Cook for 2-3 minutes per side, or until nicely charred and crispy.
To make the peanut sauce, whisk together peanut butter, soy sauce, maple syrup, rice vinegar, sesame oil, and sriracha sauce (if using) in a small bowl. Add water as needed to thin the sauce to your desired consistency.
To assemble the bowl, divide the cooked rice among four bowls. Top with grilled tempeh, kimchi, shredded carrots, shredded cabbage, and chopped peanuts. Drizzle the peanut sauce over the top of each bowl and garnish with fresh cilantro leaves.
Enjoy your delicious and healthy rice bliss bowl!

Sesame Vegan Sushi

Ingredients:

2 cups sushi rice
2 1/2 cups water
1/4 cup rice vinegar
1 tablespoon sugar
1 teaspoon salt
4 sheets of nori seaweed
1 avocado, sliced
1/2 cup sliced cucumber
1/2 cup sliced carrots
1/4 cup sliced scallions
1 tablespoon toasted sesame seeds
Soy sauce, wasabi, and pickled ginger for serving

Instructions:

Rinse the sushi rice in cold water until the water runs clear.
In a medium saucepan, combine the rinsed rice and water. Bring to a boil, then reduce the heat to low, cover, and simmer for 18-20 minutes or until the rice is tender and the water has been absorbed.
In a small bowl, whisk together the rice vinegar, sugar, and salt until the sugar and salt have dissolved.
Once the rice is cooked, transfer it to a large bowl and add the rice vinegar mixture. Stir gently to combine.
Lay a sheet of nori seaweed on a clean surface. Place a small amount of rice on the nori, leaving a 1-inch border at the top edge.
Add a few slices of avocado, cucumber, carrots, and scallions to the center of the rice.
Roll the sushi tightly, using the border of rice at the top edge to seal the roll.
Repeat with the remaining ingredients.
Slice the sushi rolls into bite-size pieces.
Sprinkle toasted sesame seeds over the sushi pieces.
Serve with soy sauce, wasabi, and pickled ginger.

This sesame vegan sushi is a healthy and delicious meal that's perfect for a light lunch or dinner. The combination of fresh vegetables, creamy avocado, and nutty sesame seeds makes for a satisfying and flavorful bite.

Taco Salad

Ingredients:
For the salad:

1 head of romaine lettuce, chopped
1 can of black beans, drained and rinsed
1 red bell pepper, chopped
1 avocado, diced
1/2 cup fresh cilantro, chopped
1/4 cup green onions, sliced
1/2 cup tortilla chips, crushed

For the taco seasoning:

1 tablespoon chili powder
1 teaspoon ground cumin
1/2 teaspoon paprika
1/4 teaspoon garlic powder
1/4 teaspoon onion powder
1/4 teaspoon dried oregano
1/4 teaspoon salt
1/4 teaspoon black pepper

For the dressing:

1/4 cup vegan sour cream
2 tablespoons fresh lime juice
1 tablespoon chopped fresh cilantro
1/4 teaspoon garlic powder
Salt and pepper to taste

Instructions:

In a small bowl, whisk together the taco seasoning ingredients.
In a large skillet over medium-high heat, add the black beans and the taco seasoning, and cook for 5-7 minutes until heated through and well-coated.
In a large bowl, combine the chopped romaine lettuce, red bell pepper, diced avocado, chopped cilantro, and sliced green onions.
Add the warm seasoned black beans to the bowl, and toss to combine.
In a small bowl, whisk together the vegan sour cream, fresh lime juice, chopped cilantro, garlic powder, salt, and pepper to make the dressing.
Drizzle the dressing over the salad, and toss to coat.
Sprinkle the crushed tortilla chips over the top of the salad.
Serve and enjoy!
This vegan taco salad is a flavorful and healthy option for any meal. The combination of crunchy vegetables, seasoned black beans, and zesty dressing is sure to satisfy your taste buds. You can also add some diced tomatoes, sliced jalapeños, or vegan cheese for some extra flavor and texture.

Vegetarian Chilli

Ingredients:

2 tablespoons olive oil
1 large onion, chopped
3 garlic cloves, minced
2 bell peppers, chopped
2 tablespoons chili powder
1 tablespoon ground cumin
1 teaspoon smoked paprika
1/2 teaspoon dried oregano
1/2 teaspoon salt
1/4 teaspoon black pepper
2 cans of kidney beans, drained and rinsed
1 can of diced tomatoes
1 cup of corn kernels
1 cup of vegetable broth
1 tablespoon soy sauce or tamari
1 tablespoon lime juice
Optional toppings: shredded cheese, chopped cilantro, sour cream or Greek yogurt, avocado

Instructions:

In a large pot or Dutch oven, heat the olive oil over medium heat.
Add the onion and garlic and cook for 5-7 minutes until softened and translucent.
Add the bell peppers and cook for another 5 minutes until softened.
Add the chili powder, cumin, smoked paprika, oregano, salt, and black pepper and stir to combine.
Add the kidney beans, diced tomatoes (with juice), corn, and vegetable broth and stir to combine.
Bring the chili to a simmer and cook for 20-25 minutes until the flavors have melded together and the chili has thickened.
Add the soy sauce or tamari and lime juice and stir to combine.
Serve the chili hot with your favorite toppings, such as shredded cheese, chopped cilantro, sour cream or Greek yogurt, or avocado.
Enjoy your vegetarian chili! It's a hearty and healthy meal that's perfect for a cozy night in.

I want to take a moment to express my heartfelt gratitude for your recent purchase of my recipe book. As a passionate food lover, nothing makes me happier than sharing my favorite recipes with others. Your decision to invest in my book not only supports my dream, but also shows your commitment to expanding your culinary horizons.

I sincerely hope that the recipes in the book will inspire you to try new things and add some excitement to your meals.

Thank you again for your support and for being a part of this journey with me. I hope my book will bring you many happy and delicious moments in the kitchen.

www.ingramcontent.com/pod-product-compliance
Lightning Source LLC
Chambersburg PA
CBHW040509110526
44587CB00044B/4144